THE FIRST FIFTY PAGES OF YOUR NOVEL

WRITING LESSONS FROM THE FRONT, BOOK 11

ANGELA HUNT

Hunt Haven Press

Visit Angela Hunt's website at www.angelahuntbooks.com.

The First Fifty Pages of Your Novel, Copyright 2023, Angela Hunt.
Published by Hunt Haven Press. All rights reserved. Do not reproduce or share
these pages without permission from the publisher.

———

Paperback ISBN: 978-1961394902, 978-1961394728
Ebook ISBN: 978-1961394162

Subscribe to Angela Hunt's newsletter for writers:
angelahunt.substack.com

WRITING LESSONS FROM THE FRONT

A Christian Writer's Possibly Useful Ruminations on a Life in Pages, supplemental volume

Paperback ISBN: 978-0692311134

Hardcover ISBN: 978-1961394100

INTRODUCTION

As of 2021, 2.3 million new books were self-published in the U.S. That's an increase of over 93% within the past five years and makes up 57.5% of the total new books published.[1]

An increase of 93 percent in the past five years . . . that's a lot of books. And most people feel that life is too short to waste time on a bad book. I know I do.

How many times have you picked up a book, read a bit, put it down . . . and never returned to it again? If you're like me, you want a book that calls to you, involves you, and keeps you turning pages.

A good writer must write a compelling book, but never is that more important than in the first fifty pages. If you don't grab a reader at the beginning, you may lose him forever.

Whether your novel will be published traditionally (a publisher pays you) or independently (you pay to have your book produced), if you want your book to succeed, if you want people to actually *read* it, you need to give your novel the absolute best chance of success. To do that, you need to work hard on your first fifty pages.

Why the first fifty? Aren't they like all the other pages?

Yes . . . and no. The first fifty pages of a novel should be specifically written to engage your reader. If they aren't, your reader might put the book down and not pick it up again . . . or not buy it in the first place. Whether a book buyer is in a store or online, readers can often read the first pages of a novel, so those pages are *extremely* significant.

By the way, there's nothing magical about the number fifty. When I refer to "your first fifty pages," I'm actually referring to the words between "Chapter One" and the point where your protagonist enters a different world and sets off on his or her grand adventure—if you were writing a play, this section would be called "Act One." In an average novel, this section is about fifty pages and will comprise the first 20-23 percent of your novel. You can determine the actual page count later.

But to keep things simple, in this lesson we're going to refer to the first fifty pages. Okay?

We are going to look at the main elements of this part of your book so you can

- 1.) Entice a book browser to become a book buyer,
- 2.) Persuade a book buyer to become a reader, and
- 3.) Convince a reader to become a loyal fan.

Ready? Here we go!

Chapter One

THE FIRST CHAPTER

As we move through this lesson, I'm going to present a hypothetical novel I'll probably never write. Let's say you've picked it up in the bookstore and opened it. Where are you heading first?

To the page labeled "Chapter One."

If you're like most people, you have flipped right past the title page, the copyright, and anything else before the first chapter. Yet many writers can't resist the urge to insert an author's note, a prologue, and acknowledgements in which they thank everyone from their spouse to their cat.

Your job as a novelist is to plunge the reader straight into the story, so why stop along the way?

If you need an author's note to explain why you adjusted a historical timeline or some other detail, put it at the back of the book.

If you want to thank those who supported you, take as many pages as you need at the back of the book.

If you want a dedication or an epigraph, keep it simple.

And why do you need a prologue? You may not need one at all. If you are *certain* you need one, keep it brief.

Whatever you do, don't compensate for a slow beginning by

stealing a scene from the ending and putting it up front as a teaser. I know that's a common situation on TV shows, but there are better ways to structure stories. Don't steal from your climax to enliven your beginning—go back and create a stronger beginning.

If you have added a prologue for the purpose of including backstory, cut it. We're not going to put backstory in the first fifty pages, because in this very important section of the book, we're interested in propelling the reader *forward*. Many writing teachers would join me in saying, "Backstory belongs at the *back* of the story."

Yes, there are exceptions to the "skip the prologue" rule. One is in the mystery genre, when a murder or other crime is often revealed in the prologue, and the first chapter opens with Mr. Detective, protagonist, reporting to work, where he deals with a problem in the office until he learns about the crime.

Another exception occurs when you wish to set the stage for your story. I crashed a plane at the beginning of my novel, *The Note*. The prologue was a brief scene written in omniscient point of view that showed various people getting onto the plane. But the reader doesn't enter the protagonist's head until chapter one.

So resist the urge to clutter up the front of your novel with stuff readers don't usually read. They want to get to the story, so let 'em get to it.

The Contract with Your Reader

Your first scene—your first chapter—establishes an unspoken contract between yourself and your reader. Without even knowing it, you are telling the reader several things about the book to come.

1. **The protagonist**: Your reader expects that the first character they meet will be the protagonist. If the character in that scene is not the novel's main character, your reader will be jarred when later they meet someone else who turns out to be the

central character. Avoid giving your reader whiplash, and let us meet your protagonist in the first scene.

Remember—good plot structure does not open with the main story event. You've probably heard that a novel should open "*in media res*," or in the middle of an action, and that's true. So show us your protagonist as he or she deals with an interesting problem in their "ordinary world."

In the introduction, I referred to the point when the protagonist enters a different world and sets off on an adventure. This should occur about 20-24 percent of the way into the story.

Have you ever seen an athlete throw a javelin? I'm no sports expert, but I've seen those athletes run down a lane, then they make a preliminary lunge before they make the throw. They initiate a smaller action before they give their all and throw the javelin.

I know that's an oversimplification, but I think it works as an analogy for story. You should open your story with a small action, an arc, that is preliminary to the larger action/arc that will become the main story problem.

Think back to *The Wizard of Oz*. In the beginning, before the tornado picks up Dorothy's house and drops her in Oz, Dorthy deals with a separate story arc—her dog has been eating Miss Gulch's flowers, so Miss Gulch demands the dog so she can take it to the sheriff. Dorothy, who lives with her aunt and uncle (nothing is ever explained about where her parents are, but there's clearly a problem), is horrified at the thought of losing her dog. She's so upset that she runs away from home and encounters a traveling fortune teller, who gazes into his crystal ball and pretends to see an older woman crying. Dorothy believes him and realizes she will hurt her aunt and uncle, so she returns home. One small story arc, one small hop, but it's all preliminary to the huge story arc that's about to unfold when the tornado picks up that house.

If you need a review on plotting, see *The Plot Skeleton*, the first book in the Writing Lessons from the Front series.

Back to our contract with the reader.

2. The first scene and chapter also identify **the genre**. The reader may have already discerned the genre by the cover, but your first scene will settle any questions. It is either a romance, a western, a mystery, a thriller, a historical, or any of the many other genres represented in bookstores. (If your book fits in none of the standard genres, it will be marketed as "general fiction.") But your first scene will reinforce the reader's impression of the genre and give them a clue about what to expect in the rest of the book.

A genre romance, for instance, always has a happy ending. The guy and the girl *will* get together. In a murder mystery, the detective will solve the crime. In a thriller, the good guy will overcome the villain. Readers read genre fiction because they know what to expect.

3. Your first scene will also establish the novel's **tense and point of view**. Tense is easy—the book is either unfolding in past tense ("He walked to the store and looked around.") or present tense (He walks to the store and looks around). Occasionally you may encounter a book that mixes tenses—for instance, a book in present tense may include a flashback written in past tense. That's appropriate. But when not writing a flashback, writers should aim for consistency so the reader isn't confused.

Point of view is a little trickier. Stories are either written in omniscient (the God-view, where a narrator relates the story and knows everything), first person (*I went to the store*), second person (*You went to the store*), or third person (*He went to the store*). Occasionally you will encounter a novel where the protagonist is written in first person and all other characters are written in third person. Whatever POV you choose, make sure your pattern is consistent. And if you need a review of *point of view* technique, the **Writing Lessons from the Front** series has a lesson on that topic.

4. The first scene and chapter also establish the **writer's voice**. What is voice? There are dozens of literary, highfalutin definitions of voice, but the reality is simple: A writer's voice is the way he or she puts words together. Each writer—indeed, each person on earth—has a way of speaking, a vocabulary, and a way of phrasing words.

The other day I had a freak out moment while watching a YouTube video. I called my agent and said, "You won't believe this, but there's a YouTuber with your voice!" It wasn't the physical sound of the woman's voice that resembled my agent's, but her vocabulary, the rhythms of her words, the pauses, even the chuckles and laughter. My agent listened to one of the videos and agreed—the resemblance was uncanny.

In the same way, every writer has a voice. The more you write, the stronger your voice grows because you become more confident. As you study craft and become more experienced, your voice will evolve, but it will always be yours. Writers who write confidently, without fear, will have strong voices.

I've had people ask, "How do I discover my voice?" The only way to discover it is to write . . . a lot. Then sit back and read some of your work aloud. Read someone else's work aloud, and notice how their voice—their rhythms, their vocabulary—differs from yours. You will each have a distinctive voice.

I remember reading one of my manuscripts that an editor had tweaked—she had inserted the word *goon*, and I laughed. In all my years of writing, I've never used that word. Not that I have anything against *goon,* goons, or goonies, but the word just isn't part of my vocabulary. Not my voice, so the word stood out.

· · ·

5. Your first scene and chapter will establish the **story world**. The reader will learn where and when the story is set, whether it's first century Rome or 25th century Mars. People in New York City speak differently than people in Atlanta, Georgia. People in Cuba *think* differently than people in the United States. Human emotions are the same no matter where or when you're writing, but the way people think, speak, work, and play can vary depending on their location, background, and worldview.

Your job in the first fifty pages is to provide a look at the daily life and social mores in your story's time and place. You don't have to describe everything—show the *top* of the iceberg, not the entire chunk of ice. And you don't have to explain.

Without explanation, how do you avoid confusing your reader? Let's say that most homes in your fictional futuristic world have a *tublinatone*. I have no idea what that would be, but you can avoid explanations by *showing the tublinatone in action*. Maybe people bathe in it. Or eat on it. Perhaps it makes music when they blow into it. Whatever you decide, don't explain it, but show people using the unfamiliar object or concept.

6. The first scene or chapter should give the reader **a hint of the ending**. You can introduce an object that will have symbolic meaning, you can feature a geographical location that will be more meaningful at the end of the novel, or you can have a character utter a phrase that will have an entirely new meaning by the end of the story. If you include a hint of the end in the beginning—and an echo of the beginning at the end—readers will feel a sense of completion when they close the book. They will have come full circle.

If you're familiar with the concept of "the hero's journey" from mythology, you'll remember that at the beginning of a story, the hero sets out on a journey. He receives a call to adventure, leaves his ordinary world and encounters a new world, sets a goal, encounters complications, experiences a bleak moment, makes a life-changing decision, and learns a lesson. He then takes his newfound maturity and knowledge and returns to his ordinary world to share what he has learned with others.

That's why it's good to hint at the ending in the beginning. You are quietly assuring your reader that things will be okay—or vastly improved—by the time the story is finished.

Chapter Two

THE FIRST LINE

"The first line sets the tone, the melody. If I hear the tone, the melody, then I have the book." (Elie Wiesel, *Against Silence: The voice and vision of Elie Wiesel*)

———

After a person picks up your book and is intrigued by the cover, he or she will then flip to the first page. The first page is home to the first scene, which features a first line.

No sentence is more important than this one.

Rare is the writer who comes up with a winning first line on the first try. I usually write five drafts of a novel, and sometimes I'm still tinkering with that first line on the fifth draft. A first line needs to be so compelling that it hooks the reader and compels them to keep reading.

Here are a few guidelines:

Avoid opening your novel with scenery.

Avoid opening your novel with descriptions of rooms or furniture.

Avoid opening your novel with a weather report.

In other words, avoid static openings.

I know, I know—you've probably read dozens of novels with static first lines about scenery, description, and weather. And while I urge you to avoid those things, I didn't say you *can't* use them. But after you've read this section, compare your current first line with descriptions of whatnot to the first line you'll write after you've read this section. Which would do a better job of hooking your reader?

Today's readers are different from yesterday's readers because we have so many more things competing for our time and attention. We have email to answer, five hundred TV stations to watch, and movies streaming on our laptops, our phones, and even our watches.

Because writers face stiff competition, they need to grab readers from the first sentence.

I'm part of an online writers' group, and frequently one of us will say, "Time to play the first line game!" and everyone will post their first sentence.

But a good many of those folks will upload two sentences, or even an entire paragraph. If you feel you need more explanation to accomplish the purpose of your first line, that sentence probably isn't pithy enough.

The best first line I've *ever* read was in a Jodi Picoult novel:

Ross Wakeman succeeded the first time he tried to kill himself, but not the second or the third. (Jodi Picoult, *Second Glance*.)

Wow. I *had* to keep reading. I don't remember what that novel was about, but I've never forgotten that first line. Why?

Let's analyze it: there's no scenery. No description. And no weather, not even a breeze.

What does it have? A person. People love to read about other people because we are social creatures who love to eavesdrop on the lives of others. The line doesn't say, "Ross Wakeman lived in sunny California . . ."

Ross Wakeman isn't interesting because he exists or because

of where he's living. He's interesting because he was trying to kill himself. And to sink that hook into the reader's psyche, Picoult adds that Ross succeeded the first time . . . but not the second or the third.

Wow. I have a half dozen questions in my head, and they are all clamoring to be answered. Why did Ross want to kill himself? If he succeeded the first time, who brought him back to life, and how? How did he try the second time . . . and the third? Why would he try again and again? And who is Ross Wakeman, anyway?

In that first line, we can find a winning first line formula. To hook a reader right away, mention **a person**, then **raise a provocative question** in the reader's mind.

I once attended an intensive writing seminar led by Don Maass, well-known writer and literary agent in New York. We students had a novel-in-progress, and Don asked each of us to stand and read our first sentence aloud. Then everyone else had to let the writer know whether or not they'd keep reading.

Talk about pressure! Don started on my side of the room, so I stood up and read mine: "A grieving woman, I've decided, is like a creme brûlée: she begins in a liquid state, endures a period of searing heat, and eventually develops a scab-like crust."

I nearly melted in relief when the others responded with smiles and nods. Why? Because I had introduced a person (the first-person narrator, who is clearly speaking from personal experience) and information that raised a question: What happened to this woman? Why was she grieving? Does she have a scab-like crust?

Some writers begin with dialogue:

"Get out of here, you horrible man!" she shrieked.

This leaves me cold, even though someone is shrieking. Why? Because I don't know this unidentified "she," and I have no idea why she's shrieking. More to the point, I don't care about this person because none of the words on the page placed me inside her head. *What* she says—"Get out of here, you horrible man"—may or may not be reliable, so it adds no dimension to the woman's character. I am a little curious about why she found a certain man horrible, but life is short and lots of things are more interesting than that question.

If you open your story with dialogue, the opening comment needs to be powerful, fascinating, and compelling.

I have just returned from my bookshelves where I opened at least a dozen beloved novels to look at their first lines. None of them opened with dialogue—not one. That doesn't mean there *aren't* any novels that effectively open with dialogue, but I couldn't find any on my overcrowded shelves. So open with dialogue *only* if it's the absolute best option you have.

I asked some of my writer friends to send me first lines from their works-in-progress—I wanted some lines that didn't sound like me. Within five minutes, I had more than I could use, so here's a sampling:

> Savannah Daniels should have known the day would be upsetting the minute she saw old Boo Radley blocking the brick walkway to her classroom.

I like that a lot—but the writer's email included a note that Boo Radley is a gator, and that's wild! Because we want to keep that sentence rhythmic and as pithy as possible, I would tweak it like this:

> Savannah Daniels should have known the day would be upsetting the minute she saw the old gator, Boo Radley, blocking the brick walkway to her classroom.

See? We have a person, Savannah Daniels, who we automatically assume to be our protagonist. We also have a challenge: an alligator is blocking Savannah's entrance to her classroom. What *is* she going to do? Plus, that sentence puts me in Savannah's head, because if seeing a gator is only "upsetting" for her, I admire her pluckiness. I'd be terrorized.

Another friend sent this one:

Nightmares were supposed to stop once little girls woke up, but when five-year-old Scarlett Radcliffe opened her eyes, things only got worse.

I like this! I'm thinking Scarlett Radcliffe is the protagonist, probably as an adult, and this feels like a suspense novel. The only edit I might make would be to change the word "things" to something more specific: "the night only got worse." Or "her situation" only got worse. Or "she discovered her nightmare had just begun." (Words like "things" and "it" are often nonspecific, and specificity works better.)

Here's another:

My gymnastics career ended with an injury—and I wasn't even the one who got hurt.

That line made me laugh. I can see that the "person" is the first person narrator, and I want to remain in her company because she made me smile. The provocative question, obviously, is who got hurt? And how in the world could that happen?

What about this one:

On July 4, 2019, a body floated just below the surface near the mouth of the Back River in Eastern Virginia.

This intriguing line reads like the beginning of a murder mystery. I'm not familiar with the story, but many suspense novels open with a dead body. The omniscient point of view presents a factual view of what's happening, but even this brief line includes a person—the body—and a provocative question: what happened to this person? And how did he or she come to be in the river? Also, notice the specificity of the date—the writer nailed it to a specific date, the Fourth of July. Interesting!

Another writer contributed this line:

> It took one-ten-thousandth of a second—exactly 0.000169 seconds—for the bullet to rip through his shoulder.

I love it. Why? Because a person—a man—is getting shot. Why? I want to know. I also want to know how he knows the exact speed at which the bullet is traveling. He's clearly some kind of expert on gunfire and/or ballistics. And talk about specificity!

I'm not familiar with this writer's story, either, but I suspect that the point of view character is either the man getting shot or a medical examiner reviewing a body. If it's the latter case, I might tweak it by adding the medical examiner's name to put the reader in her point of view, like this: "Allison Wendel noted that it had taken one-tenth of a second—exactly 0.00169 seconds—for the bullet to rip through the man's shoulder."

But if the POV character is the man being shot, that line is perfect just as it is.

And one more:

> Cemeteries always smelled of earthworms and damp dog fur, especially after a rain, and Brudge rather liked it that way.

Oh. My. Goodness. This is beautifully creepy, and though I don't know who Brudge is—or even if Brudge is a he or a she—I'm hooked. Who is this person, and why does he like the smell of cemeteries? What has happened in his past? People aren't born with a love for rainy, smelly cemeteries.

So when you begin your novel, write your first scene and get on with the novel. Don't let your progress come to a complete stop over a single sentence.

But keep coming back to that first line. Polish it again and again. Run it past your friends. Cut words, add words, read it aloud and listen to the rhythm. Cut any extra syllables. Make the verbs unexpected. Add specific sound, smells, tastes. Make sure there's a person for the reader to care about, and a question that entices the reader to keep reading.

Practice makes perfect.

Chapter Three

THE FIRST SCENE

Since nearly every new writer knows the first scene should start with some kind of action, many begin the story with an explosion, a gunfight, a murder, or a kidnapping.

Those things are okay if you're writing a thriller or a western, but what if you're writing women's fiction? And even if you're writing a thriller about child who is kidnapped, why shouldn't you begin with the kidnapping?

Let me show you:

On a cloudy Friday morning in June, nine-year-old Louisa Jones's life changed at the corner of Wimple Avenue and South State Street. She waited on the sidewalk, book bag in hand, for the stubborn light to change. Without warning, a black van whipped around the corner and stopped, its door sliding open with a slam. A masked man jumped out, grabbed Louisa, and threw her into the van. The driver slammed on the gas, the van rocketed into the right lane, and the startled onlookers stared in horror.

Only when one of them noticed the girl's plaid book bag on the sidewalk did someone think to call the police.

Nice first sentence, huh? Much better than the one I had in my first draft.

But this opening isn't nearly as effective as it should be because we don't care much about Louisa. How can we? We don't know her.

The average reader has read hundreds of newspaper stories about abandoned, abused, and missing children, and we've grown accustomed to the fact that evil exists in our world. We don't like it, but we are no longer horrified or shocked by it.

So how do we bring the horror of Louisa's situation home to the reader?

Here's the technique: we create a "short hop" story arc that will do all the things we've outlined in the contract with the reader. The true purpose of this small arc is to illustrate Louisa's character so the reader will care about her when the short story arc ends and the main story problem begins.

So let's say Louisa wants to enroll in space camp for kids, and she thinks her dad might not let her because she's only nine. But she loves anything to do with space travel, and she wants to be an astronaut when she grows up. So she's trying to find the courage and the right time to approach her father.

And here's the backstory—which we're not going to write or explain, but we're going to allow it to ripple beneath the scenes like a dark current.

Three years before, while the family was on vacation in Florida, Louisa's mother saved six-year-old Louisa from a riptide, but couldn't get back to shore. She drowned, Louisa's father busied himself with work to avoid confronting his grief, and ever since Louisa has been attended by a series of nannies. The family is wealthy and lives in a large urban city.

While we're constructing the "short hop" plot, the reader needs to bond with Louisa. We need to help the reader feel her emotions. Because this is a kidnapping story, Louisa is going to feel dread and fear.

Because every writer is a former child, we should be able to remember what fear feels like. So make a list of every occasion you can remember being terrified. What did you do when you were anxious? What do you do now when you're nervous? What did you do as a child? This exercise will help Louisa experience the same dread, fear, and worry you felt when you were younger.

Now that we have a small story arc, instead of opening with the abduction, we can open with Louisa in her ordinary world. She has a goal—space camp—and problems readers can relate to.

In this first scene, she's running late for school. How do you react when you're running late?

Louisa pulled on her cardigan and stared into the mirror, then licked her fingertip and ran her damp finger over the rebellious cowlick near her forehead. Her mother used to do that, and Louisa never minded the touch of her wet fingers.

"Louisa!" A voice called from the bottom of the staircase. "Hurry up, you're making me late!"

Louisa sighed and looked for her shoes. One lay next to the bed where she'd kicked it off the night before, but the other?

She dropped and peered beneath the bed. Nothing.

She stood and searched the closet. Nothing.

"Louisa!" The voice was harder now. "For the last time, get down here!"

Louisa bit her lip, then remembered that Jasper had been in her room and the puppy had a thing for shoes. She put on her right shoe and padded down the hallway to the bathroom, where Jasper was put away at night.

There—her shoe lay in his bed, a little chewed, but not too much.

She slipped it on, patted the puppy's head, then ran back to her room and grabbed her book bag.

"Louisa, I'm coming up there! You won't like it if I catch you!"

Louisa strode toward the door, then stopped to kiss two fingers and press them to the picture that stood on her dresser.

In the fading photo she and her mother stood on the beach, both of them smiling into the camera.

Louisa rushed toward the stairs, wondering if she would ever be that happy again.

Okay—see how this short scene gives us insight into Louisa's life? The woman at the foot of the stairs is obviously not Louisa's mother. She doesn't sound very kind or caring, and Louisa is intimidated enough not to yell back at the woman.

Louisa isn't causing a problem on purpose—anyone who has a dog has dealt with missing shoes, so the problem isn't Louisa's fault. But it's distressing for Louisa because the woman keeps yelling, and it's also distressing for the reader. We feel for the kid, and when we see that she pauses to press a kiss to the photo, we realize something awful has happened to Louisa's mother. The beach hints at the drowning, but this isn't fully revealed yet.

Notice that we did not take the time to explain anything— we didn't explain who the woman was, where and when the photo was taken, or what happened to Louisa's mother. Our job in the first fifty pages is to *resist the urge to explain*, or RUE. Our job is to propel the story forward and create questions in the reader's mind. When we do that, we are creating tension, not of the mad bomber variety, but of character.

The woman downstairs grows ever more impatient, but Louisa bears the woman's sharpness in silence. Will she explode? Will she remonstrate? Will she ever fight back?

Notice that there are no recollections or flashbacks in the scene. For our purposes, a recollection is a *brief memory within a scene that takes place in past story time*. A flashback is *a complete and separate scene set in past story time*.

We could have inserted a recollection when Louisa paused to kiss the photo:

Louisa strode toward the door, then stopped to kiss her fingers and press her hand to the picture that stood on her dresser. In the aging photo she and her mother stood on the beach, both of them smiling into the camera.

That **had** been the last time they visited Indian Rocks Beach and stayed at the little vacation house. Mom and Dad were happy, laughing and singing and swimming in the warm gulf. They **had** gathered shells and roasted marshmallows on the shore . . . a memory that remained with Louisa even now.

Louisa rushed toward the stairs, wondering if she would ever be that happy again.

Nothing is technically wrong with that recollection, but even though it's short, the recollection stops the story in its tracks. The stop would be even worse if the recollection had been longer. And why is it necessary? The reader doesn't need to know where they were staying or that they roasted marshmallows. All the reader needs to know is that the woman in the photo is Louisa's mother, and that Louisa loves and misses her. That information informs the reader about the woman yelling at the foot of the stairs. We don't know who she is—she could be a nanny, a distant relative, a housekeeper, or a stepmother—but we will drop other hints later.

Your goal in the first fifty pages is to eliminate all backstory. I know it's tough, but try to aim for no back story in *at least* the first thirty pages. You and your reader will be glad you did.

So if you've written your first draft, go through the first section and highlight anything, however short, that takes place *prior to the present story moment.* Then create a new computer file, name it "Cut backstory," and cut/paste your backstory sections into that file. I know it's painful to cut material, but don't worry. You're not trashing it, you're simply stowing it somewhere else. It'll be there if you need it, but I'm pretty sure you won't.

Here's a tip about how to find bits of backstory in your text. Go to the "edit" menu and select the search/replace function. Search for "had" and replace it with "HAD" in capital letters.

Now you're likely to see your backstory bits bookended by "hads."

Look at the example above, about Louisa and her mother on Indian Rocks beach. The proper way to introduce a recollection is by the use of "had"—you use one at the beginning of the recollection to take the reader back, and you use another at the end of the recollection to bring the reader back to present story time. You only need two *hads*—you don't need to use past perfect tense within the recollection.

So cut the backstory, save it in your backstory file, and read your draft again. I'm betting that it reads better because the story is only moving in one direction—forward. Don't worry—if you've cut explanatory material and you feel it's important, there are other ways to work it in—through dialogue, perhaps, or through exposition. But use those methods logically, and don't fall for the old trap of "As you know, Bob." If you have one character telling another character what the second character would already know, back up and start again.

If I had the woman at the bottom of the stairs saying, "As you know, Louisa, I've been your nanny for three years, ever since your mama drowned off that beach in Florida," well—that's an "as you know, Bob." Kill it. You don't need it.

So how would you get some of that information to the reader? Perhaps like this:

> When the BWM stopped at the corner, the woman behind the wheel stopped chewing her gum long enough to stare at Louisa. "What 'cha waiting for, kid? Outta the car."
>
> Louisa unlocked the door, grabbed her book bag, and hopped out. She turned, about to say goodbye, but the BMW was already rolling, barely giving her time to close the door.
>
> Louisa's friend Amanda waited by the bike rack in front of Starbucks. "Hey, Louisa."
>
> "Hi."

Amanda cracked a gap-toothed smile. "How was the witch this morning?"

Louisa blew out a breath. "About the same."

"How many nannies have you had since—you know."

"Four. Not counting this one."

"Wow." Amanda rummaged in her book bag, then pulled out a bag of fruit snacks. "Here. 'Cause I know you don't get sweets in your bag." She waited until Louisa ripped the package open with her teeth, then grinned. "So? Did you ask your dad?"

Louisa popped a fruit snack into her mouth and blinked. "About?"

"Space camp. The deadline's next week."

"I know. But—" Louisa sighed. "I don't think he's going to let me. He'll say I'm too young."

"But Mr. Martin said you'd qualify 'cause of your good grades. And I don't want to go by myself."

Louisa looked up at the sky, where a scattering of cumulous clouds reminded her of last night's popcorn. "I'm going to ask," she said, lowering her gaze. "When the time is right."

"You better find the right time soon." Amanda crossed her arms over her book bag. "Because I can't go to space camp without my best friend."

See? You can get whatever explanations you need to give the reader in present story time. Just *keep the story moving forward*. There will be a time for looking back—and a reason—later.

Chapter Four

THE READER-CHARACTER BOND

As a novelist, your job is to create a bond between the reader and your protagonist. Before we discover how that can be done, let's refresh our knowledge of story structure.

If you've read *The Plot Skeleton*, you may remember that the "inciting incident"—the big event that happens when the protagonist moves into a different world—usually happens about 20 percent of the way into the story. In a two hour movie, that's usually around 22-24 minutes into the film. That's the point where Maria leaves the convent to work at the Von Trapp family mansion (*The Sound of Music*), where the tornado picks up Dorothy's house and deposits her in Oz (*The Wizard of Oz*), and where the Bruce Willis character discovers there are terrorists in the high rise (*Die Hard*). In our story, this will be when Louisa is kidnapped, because that's the event that will move the story in another direction and Louisa will unwillingly enter a different world.

The first part of your story—the first 20 percent or so—is where you develop your character so the reader is happy to travel with the protagonist into what can be a frightening and unfamiliar new world. In order for the reader to agree to the adventure, you have about fifty pages to create a bond between your reader and your protagonist.

If I wanted the protagonist of this book to be a detective, I would have opened the story with a scene from the detective's point of view. He would have been dealing with a problem—maybe he gets an emergency call and his car won't start—and I would have included details to reveal *his* character and hint at his backstory.

If I wanted the protagonist of this kidnapping story to be the girl's worried father, I would have opened the book with a scene from the father's point of view. He would have been dealing with an interesting problem and a small goal—perhaps he was robbed of his wallet by a thirteen-year-old hoodlum, which sends him to the police station to complain about rising crime while oblivious to the danger awaiting his own daughter.

But my plan is for Louisa to be a bright, admirable, science-loving girl who engineers her own rescue from the diabolical kidnappers. In order to make this idea credible, in the first act of the story I have to provide the reader with evidence that Louisa *might* be able to manage this feat. I wouldn't want to make it a certainty, or I'd wipe out all the tension in the story. But I don't want her to inexplicably turn into a whiz kid, either.

In an 80,000 word book, that means I have about 16,000 words, or approximately 64 pages, to show that Louisa is capable, smart, and resourceful.

So I will need to construct scenes that demonstrate those qualities while she pursues her small goal of persuading her father to let her attend space camp. I have to write scenes that show her vulnerability. I should probably introduce suspects who could engineer this kidnapping. I ought to introduce the important people in her life—her father, the nanny, her best friend, her favorite teacher, the boy she likes best, and her beloved dog.

I might want to lay the groundwork for the villains, give them a reasonable motive for the kidnapping, and hint at what they will do if her father doesn't pay the ransom. I should introduce a few "red herrings," or likely suspects—the nanny is a natural for this role, since I've already painted her as unlikeable.

But most important, whether the main character is the detective, the father, or the kidnapped girl, I have to make the reader love with my protagonist. How?

1. Make your protagonist **vulnerable**. It's easy to make a child vulnerable, but what if your protagonist is a strong, capable man? Most police procedurals and movies exploit the detective's vulnerability by threatening someone he loves—his wife, his family, or his dog. Love puts all of us at risk, doesn't it?

You could also make your protagonist vulnerable by giving him a physical handicap—debilitating migraines, for instance, blindness, deafness, or a broken leg. The vulnerability could be permanent, or something that comes and goes. But your protagonist must have a vulnerability. Even Superman has kryptonite.

2. Make your protagonist **admirable and competent**. Give him a noble nature. Give him physical and/or moral strength and convictions. Make her virtuous or spiritual. Give her a special talent or ability, something no one else can do as well as she can. Make this gift surprising—a strong man who saves abandoned kittens or a woman who can fix a car better than the neighborhood mechanic.

Even antiheroes have to be admirable in some way. In *The Godfather*, Don Corleone ran a crime syndicate and had people murdered, but he had a code of ethics—his organization refused to sell drugs. Bad for the kids, they said. And while you're creating an antagonist or villain, remember that he need to have a good reason for doing the evil he does. His machinations may not make sense to the rest of the world, but they make sense to your villain.

4. Give your protagonist a **flaw**. It doesn't have to be huge—it could be as simple as a tendency to do things halfway. Or perhaps he tells one little "white lie." Or she betrays one friend. Whatever it is, this flaw or weakness will eventually come around to bite them, and they'll learn a lesson. We all have flaws,

and we've all learned from them. Your reader will identify more easily with a less-than-perfect character than a superhero.

5. Give your protagonist a **sense of humor**—especially if it's self-deprecating. If you're creating an interesting, gifted, smart character, give them a little humility to counteract all those strengths. Let her shrug off her victories. Let him sincerely celebrate when others win. Allow him to point out his weaknesses and failings. Make your protagonist fully human. If you're familiar with the Myers-Briggs personality profiles, give your protagonist a type and you'll be able to research his strengths and weaknesses in a flash.

6. Give your character **a hidden need**. This is not the same thing as a flaw—a flaw can be trivial, but the hidden need is deeply emotional and usually the result of some wound in the protagonist's past. This wound may not be easy to spot—after all, it's hidden in the first fifty pages—but you should give evidence that it exists.

Picture a circle with points at the top and bottom. The top point represents the beginning of the story, and the bottom point represents the end of the story. The right side of the circle represents the plot movement, and the left side character movement.

A good story has active plot and active character development, but some stories place more weight on one side than the other. *Steel Magnolias* is a character-driven story about a woman, M'Lynn, who struggles to save her daughter's life while depending on the support of her friends. The plot is centered on all the things M'Lynn does while trying to save her daughter (stop Shelby's wedding, stop her from having children, arranging for a kidney transplant), while the character growth is centered on how M'Lynn learns to deal with letting her child go her own way . . . and learning that life goes on even after a loved one dies.

Most James Bond films, on the other hand, are heavily weighted on the *plot* side of the circle. Agent 007 works against impossible odds to save the world from a nefarious villain while remaining unflappable . . . except in the last few movies, where he's actually been allowed to express a few emotions.

Try to make sure both sides of the circle are well-represented in your novel. By the end of the novel, the hidden emotional need you've portrayed in the first fifty pages should be met and the wound healed. Your protagonist is now changed for the better. He will either live happily ever after, or be sadder and wiser.

7. Finally, recall your own experiences and **transfer your past emotions** to your characters. How did you feel when your best friend discovered you'd leaked the secret you promised not to tell? How did you feel when your mom forgot your birthday? How did you react when you didn't win a ribbon at the county science fair? How do you react when you're in a hurry and your car won't start? Let your protagonist feel those feelings and your readers will relate to your character. Because at one time or another, they've felt the same emotions.

Remember Dorothy's small story arc at the beginning of the Wizard of Oz? If you haven't watched the movie lately, pull it out, watch it, and then consider the reasons we bond with Dorothy in that first arc of the story:

1. We see that she's loyal, brave, and sacrificial. She fights for her dog, Toto, and would willingly go to bed without supper for him.

2. She's vulnerable. She's living with her aunt and uncle, with no sign of her parents.

3. She's virtuous—we see her being kind and friendly with the farm hands, who are obviously fond of her.

4. She's talented—in the movie, she sings beautifully.

5. She's devoted to her family—when she runs away, all Professor Marvel has to do is point out that Auntie Em would miss her, and Dorothy hurries home. She doesn't want to hurt anyone.

6. She has dreams and longings and feels fierce emotions.

Wouldn't we rather read about a passionate person than someone who's apathetic?

7. She has a hidden need—since her parents are gone, she needs to feel that she's home on her aunt and uncle's farm. In the first act, we see that she's living with relatives who aren't her parents, but we know she's not happy because she longs to live "somewhere over the rainbow." After being separated from her relatives and trapped in Oz, she is desperate to return to the Kansas farm to live with Uncle Henry and Auntie Em. She learns that "there's no place like home."

So if you've been wondering how you're going to fill up those first fifty pages, here's your answer. Create scenes and situations in which your protagonist reveals virtues, weaknesses, a hidden need, talents, dreams and goals, and vulnerability. Help him or her strive toward a small goal, encounter a couple of problems, and overcome them. Then they'll be ready for the major inciting incident, which will carry them into a new world with a much larger goal and subsequent problems.

If you can do those things in the first fifty pages, you've given your protagonist everything he or she needs to appeal to a reader.

Chapter Five

THE BACKSTORY

A fully-fleshed character has a backstory: the sum total of the life events that have shaped her to become the person she is. So as you work on your novel, ask yourself this question: What is the single most transformative event in my protagonist's life before chapter one begins?

For Louisa, my young protagonist, it would be her mother's drowning on their family vacation. Louisa is nine years old when the story opens; the drowning occurred when she was six. Six is old enough to remember a catastrophic event.

If I had chosen the father or detective as the protagonist, I would have many more choices because adults have lived far longer than nine-year-old Louisa. Perhaps the father's most formative life event was when he defied his father and chose to go to law school and not take over the family business. This disagreement has colored his family relationships ever since.

Perhaps the detective's formative event occurred when he was thirteen and his best friend was hit by a car. The reckless driver was never identified, so since then the detective has yearned to "set things right." His loss changed his life and directly influenced his decision to join the police force.

Once you've decided on a formative event, ask yourself how

lessons the protagonist learned during that time could affect him as your story unfolds. Since we're going to avoid backstory in the first section of the novel, once your hero has entered the special story world (*after* the first fifty pages), you can be more open and include references to that event from years past. Don't reveal it all at once, though.

At one point, probably around the three-quarter point in the novel, you could insert a flashback and give us an entire scene of the event as it happened in your character's life. Don't short-change this one by making it a brief recollection. Give us the entire scene, complete with sights, sounds, tastes, textures, and raw emotions.

Your reader will now understand why your protagonist feels, acts, and reacts the way he or she does . . . because they, too, have lived through that transformative event.

But don't drop this flashback on page fifty-one. Save it for the moment your protagonist is about to face the biggest challenge of his story. After the flashback scene, he will own the memories, emotions, and lessons of that life-changing event, broaden his shoulders, and charge forward to win or lose.

There is a time—late in the story—for backstory. But it needs to be *significant* backstory, not meaningless details.

I'm not saying that you can use *only* backstory of the most transformative event—our lives are changed by myriad meaningful moments, and you can use any of them. If writing about adults, consider the moments they fell in love, got married, got divorced, grieved a death, suffered disappointment, won an unlikely victory, or became a parent. Memories from any of those or similar events will deepen character when you allow us to experience them through the eyes of your protagonist. So feel free to delve into your characters' pasts to allow the reader to realize why your characters are the way they are. Just try your best to keep all those memories, recollections, and flashbacks out of the first part of your story.

Everything in your novel should do one of two things:

advance the story forward or deepen characterization. If an element isn't pulling its weight, cut it and stash it in a file. You don't need it, and you probably won't miss it.

Your reader certainly won't.

Chapter Six

THE BOOK'S COVER

If your novel will be traditionally published, you won't have to be overly concerned about the cover. I hesitated to include this section because a book's cover isn't really part of the first fifty pages, but if our goal is to hook a reader in a bookstore, the cover certainly plays an important part. The cover is especially important if you plan to self-publish your novel—you will be the publisher, so you will have to make sure the cover attracts your ideal reader.

What does a prospective reader see first in a typical bookstore or on a library shelf? The book **spine**, of course, unless the book is displayed face out. The writer can't do much about what's on the spine (unless you're designing the spine yourself), but the title and author's name should be clearly displayed.

The second—and most important—element a prospective reader sees is the **front cover.** Fortunately, online book buyers see the cover first, and that's a good thing because the cover should entice a book buyer by clearly indicating the the title and the author's name. The artwork, whether complex or simple, should give a clue as to genre—you would not expect a murder mystery to feature the flowers and soft colors of a women's fiction novel. You would not expect a contemporary novel to feature women in long skirts and upswept Victorian hairstyles.

If you're writing your first or second book, you'll probably want to put your title at the top of the cover. Make sure it's a good title, and put your name beneath it. Your readers will be attracted to the book because of the cover, the title, and the concept because they don't know you—yet.

If you develop a strong readership, you can put your name at the top. By that time readers should be drawn to *you*. This isn't a hard and fast rule, but if you browse a bookstore, you'll see that best-selling writers have their names featured first . . .because readers are drawn to the author, not the title.

If you are designing your own book cover or giving direction to a graphic artist, study book covers in your genre and utilize the same conventions. I'm not saying you should copy another writer's cover, but you would want to avoid a style that is dramatically different from other books in the genre.

Covers images do tend to trend, so do an internet search for "book cover trends" and you'll find ideas that are currently well-received in various genres. Handwriting fonts are popular at the time of this writing, but the font should be legible from a distance. Also remember to use no more than two different fonts on the cover, otherwise the type begins to look disorganized and jumbled. If one font is fancy and has lots of serifs and swirls, make the other font non serif and simple. The two should compliment with contrast.

Note: limit yourself to two fonts, but it's fine to use standard *and* italics or bold versions of the same font if you need some variety.

One word of advice: don't *ever* use the Comic Sans Serif font on a book cover. Nothing makes a cover look more amateur.

Once you have created a mockup of the cover, reduce the size to a thumbnail, and make sure the text is still legible and that the image hasn't become murky. Your book may be a small image in an ad or at an online bookstore, so the details in the design may disappear. Your cover needs to work when it's full size as well as when it's a thumbnail.

If your publisher is designing the book cover, be sure to give them ideas about what you feel would work. Most traditional publishers send out a "cover questionnaire" for you to fill out even before you hand in the manuscript. Keep in mind that the cover artist will probably not read your book, so let the art department know what your protagonist looks like by indicating hair and eye color along with any distinguishing physical characteristics. Some genres almost always feature the protagonist on the cover; other genres rarely do. Study books in your genre so you know what is expected.

You may have a cover in mind, but do be open to new ideas.

Recently I finished a book of advent devotions and designed a mock up cover to submit to my publisher—it was light and bright and beautiful. My publisher had a different idea, and sent me a mockup that was detailed and dark. I disliked it at first, probably because it was the opposite of what the cover I had in mind.

So I went to my Facebook page and uploaded two images—the dark cover and the exact opposite, with the colors reversed—all the darks were light, and all the lights were dark. Then I asked my Facebook followers which cover they preferred.

Within minutes, I learned I was wrong. Out of more than a hundred respondents, only one liked the light version better. The artist's work was beautiful, and the reaction of unbiased readers confirmed that for me.

So if your publisher designs a cover for your book, be open-minded, but do speak up about obvious errors. If you've written about a beautiful brunette, ask for a correction if the artist has portrayed a beautiful blonde.

Here's a tip about covers: you wouldn't want to do this in *every* cover, of course, but if your cover should feature your protagonist, try to find or create an image in which the character *looks out into the eyes* of the reader. There's something compelling about looking at a book and seeing the character look back at you.

After a prospective book buyer has been intrigued by the cover, he or she will flip the book over and read the **back cover copy.** I always submit my manuscripts with a couple of paragraphs of sample back cover copy, because no one knows the book like I do. My publisher may use my copy, tweak it, or write new copy altogether. You may know your book, but your publisher knows the market, so if they have sound reasons for changing your copy, listen to them. Effective back cover copy is important.

Back cover copy (which is often used on an online bookstore's page) is the next step in enticing a prospective book buyer. It should give a clear idea of what the book is about, but it should not spoil any plot events or reveal the ending. The back cover copy should raise questions in the reader's mind that demand to be answered, compelling the buyer to read the book.

Much of what is featured on the cover is out of the writer's hands, especially if published by a traditional publisher. These publishers have experienced marketers and designers and art departments who will use their skills to create an effective cover.

If you are publishing your book yourself, it's your responsibility to make your cover the best it can be.

Several years ago, a friend and I were at a writer's conference sitting in the "book room," where conferees and speakers had books for purchase. As we looked out over the tables, we realized we could tell at a glance which books had been self-published. How? Because the covers just weren't as good as those from traditional publishers.

When I first began to self-publish digital editions of some of my out of print books, I thought it was as easy as grabbing a piece of stock art, adding my title and byline, and putting back cover copy on the back. Some of my early cover efforts were absolutely awful.

But then I took a simple online class in graphic design, and once I applied the principles I learned, my covers improved dramatically. I also began to use quality stock photos purchased from online stock photo vendors, not the "free graphics" available online. Now I design most of my self-published covers, but it took time to learn design principles and Photoshop techniques.

By the way—just because a photo is online does not mean you have permission to use it for your blog, your book cover, or your newsletter. Photos are copyrighted by the person who took it (the photographer), and you are violating copyright if you use it without permission or a license. Even some "free" photos have stipulations, so be sure to read the fine print. If you plan on selling a product that features an image, you may have to purchase a commercial license. Some photographers hire agencies to search the Internet for authorized use of their images, so if you don't properly procure a license, you could find yourself liable for penalties and fees.

———

In summary, when designing a book cover, keep these four principles in mind:

1.) **Contrast**: if using a bold, businesslike font for the title, use something softer for the author's name. Also use contrasting colors when appropriate.

2.) **Clarity**: Most people read from left to right, so don't split up text in little bunches around parts of the featured image. Keep groups of related text together (all the back cover copy, for instance), and don't spread it out. Keep the cover clean and simple, with only necessary ingredients.

3.) **Proximity**: If you want to add "Award-Winning Author" to the cover (if that is true), keep it near the author's name. In other words, keep related text together.

4.) **Alignment**: Design the front, spine, and back together, as one image—you can always crop the front image for display. Make sure that paragraphs of text are evenly spaced with clean edges.

EXERCISES

1, Your first sentence—come up with five possible first sentences for your book. Make sure at least one of them has a person and something that will raise a question in the reader's mind. Try them out on some potential readers . . . or passersby. Which one works best for them?

2. Your first chapter: did you make the common mistake of beginning with the main problem of the book? If you did, move it forward a few chapters and start again, opening with your protagonist dealing with an obvious problem. Make sure we get to know and like this character as he or she deals with the problem. This first part of the book is all about developing a bond between protagonist and reader.

3. Check your first fifty pages for ANY bits of backstory—any reference to an event that occurred before the present story time. Highlight those lines and/or paragraphs and cut them, placing them in a folder you can name "Backstory." Now continue with your story, knowing that the cut material is there if you need it . . . but you probably won't. Doesn't your story move faster without all that backstory in it? Backstory belongs at the back of the story, when you're finally ready to reveal the

event that has made your character the flawed person he or she is.

4. Find a copy of a contemporary novel you really enjoyed. Now skim through the beginning and find the inciting incident —when the real story problem kicks off. What has the author used to get the reader to that point? What did he or she use to increase the bond between you, the reader, and his protagonist? Try to use some of those same techniques in your work in progress.

THANK YOU!

Now it's time to put this lesson down and get to work on your first fifty pages!

I hope this lesson has proved helpful for you. If you need help with an area of writing not covered by any other other **Writing Lessons from the Front**,[1] contact me through my website and I'll see what I can do to help!

We would appreciate it if you would be kind enough to leave a review of this book on Amazon. Thank you!

A huge thanks to Thomas Umstattd, Jr., who first talked with me about the *First Fifty Pages* on his **Novel Marketing Podcast**, the longest-running book marketing podcast in the world. This is *the* show for writers who want to build their platform, sell more books, and change the world with writing worth talking about. Whether you self publish or are with a traditional house, this podcast will make book promotion fun and easy. Thomas Umstattd Jr. interviews publishers, indie authors, and bestselling traditional authors about how to get published and sell more books.

Learn more about the podcast at https://www.authormedia.com/novel-marketing/

NOTES

INTRODUCTION

1. Chris Kolmar, 23 Gripping Book Industry Statistics {2023}: Average Book Sales Over Time and by Genre https://www.zippia.com/advice/us-book-industry-statistics/, accessed May 24, 2023.

THANK YOU!

1. Writing Lessons from the Front, the first ten books: https://www.amazon.com/Writing-Lessons-Front-First-Books-ebook/dp/B00OD-CK9HA/ref=sr_1_1?crid=26SZSQJQoHAIA&keywords=writing+lessons+from+the+front&qid=1684964364&sprefix=writing+lessons+from+the+front%2Caps%2C143&sr=8-1

ABOUT THE AUTHOR

Angela Hunt writes for readers who have learned to expect the unexpected from this versatile writer. With nearly six million copies of her books sold worldwide, she is the best-selling author of more than 165 works ranging from picture books (*The Tale of Three Trees*) to novels and nonfiction.

Now that her two children are grown, Angie and her husband live in Florida with Very Big Dogs (a direct result of watching *Turner and Hooch* too many times) and many chickens. Her affinity for mastiffs has not been without its rewards—one of their dogs was featured on *Live with Regis and Kelly* as the second-largest canine in America. Their dog received this dubious honor after an all-expenses-paid trip to Manhattan for the dog and the Hunts, complete with VIP air travel and a stretch limo in which they toured New York City. Afterward, the dog gave out pawtographs at the airport.

Angela admits to being fascinated by animals, medicine, unexplained phenomena, and "just about everything." Books, she says, have always shaped her life— in the fifth grade she learned how to flirt from reading *Gone with the Wind*.

Her books have won the coveted Christy Award, several Angel Awards from Excellence in Media, and the Gold and Silver Medallions from *Foreword Magazine*'s Book of the Year Award. In 2007, her novel *The Note* was featured as a Christmas movie on the Hallmark channel.

When she's not home writing, Angie often travels to teach

writing workshops at schools and writers' conferences. And to talk about her animals, of course. Readers may visit her web site at www.angelahuntbooks.com.

f **☉**

www.ingramcontent.com/pod-product-compliance
Lightning Source LLC
Chambersburg PA
CBHW070031030426

42335CB00017B/2391